ALLERGY FREE RECIPES FOR KIDS

By : Naomi Hastings

What is Food Allergy?

A food allergy is when your immune system reacts to certain foods, causing symptoms like rashes, stomach issues, or, in severe cases, trouble breathing. Common allergens include peanuts, milk, and eggs. Some reactions can be serious and need immediate medical help.

EGG FREE

Spinach and Feta Stuffed Peppers Recipe

Servings: 4

45 minutes

Ingredients

- 4 large bell peppers

- 1 cup cooked rice

- 2 cups fresh spinach, chopped

- 1 cup crumbled feta cheese

- 1 cup tomato sauce

- 1 tablespoon olive oil

- 1 teaspoon dried oregano

- Salt and pepper to taste

Tools

- Baking dish

- Mixing bowls

- Cutting board

- Knife

- Spoon

- Oven

Instructions

1. Preheat your oven to 375°F (190°C).

2. Cut the tops off the bell peppers, remove seeds, and place them in a baking dish.

3. Heat olive oil in a pan. Add chopped spinach and sauté until wilted.

4. In a bowl, mix cooked rice, sautéed spinach, feta, oregano, salt, and pepper.

5. Stuff each pepper with this mixture.

6. Pour tomato sauce over the stuffed peppers.

7. Cover the dish with foil and bake for 25 minutes or until peppers are tender.

8. Remove the foil and bake for an extra 5 minutes to get a nice top layer.

9. Allow the peppers to cool a bit before serving.

Enjoy these easy Spinach and Feta Stuffed Peppers – a tasty, veggie-packed dish that's simple to make!

Tomato Basil Grilled Cheese Recipe

2 servings

20 minutes

Ingredients

- 4 slices of bread

- 8 slices of ripe tomato

- Fresh basil leaves

- 1 1/2 cups shredded mozzarella cheese

- Butter (for spreading)

- Salt and pepper to taste

Tools

- Griddle or skillet

- Spatula

Instructions

1. Place a griddle or skillet over medium heat.

2. Lay out the slices of bread.

3. Butter one side of each slice.

4. On the non-buttered side of two slices, evenly distribute the mozzarella cheese.

5. Place 4 tomato slices on top of the cheese on each slice.

6. Add fresh basil leaves over the tomatoes.

7. Sprinkle a pinch of salt and pepper over the tomatoes and basil.

8. Top each with another slice of bread, buttered side facing out.

9. Place the sandwiches on the heated griddle or skillet.

10. Cook until the bread is golden brown, and the cheese is melted (about 3-4 minutes per side).

11. Carefully flip the sandwiches with a spatula and cook the other side until golden brown.

12. Once both sides are golden and the cheese is melted, remove from the heat.

13. Allow the sandwiches to cool for a minute before slicing.

14. Serve warm and enjoy your delicious Tomato Basil Grilled Cheese!

Mushroom and Spinach Pizza Recipe

2-4 servings

30 minutes

Ingredients

- 1 pizza dough (store-bought or homemade)

- 1/2 cup pizza sauce

- 1 1/2 cups shredded mozzarella cheese

- 1 cup sliced mushrooms

- 2 cups fresh spinach leaves, washed and dried

- 1 tablespoon olive oil

- 2 cloves garlic, minced

- Salt and pepper to taste

- Red pepper flakes (optional, for added spice)

Tools

- Pizza stone or baking sheet

- Rolling pin (if the dough needs rolling)

- Pizza cutter or sharp knife

Instructions

1. Preheat your oven to the temperature specified on the pizza dough package or your homemade dough recipe.

2. Roll out the pizza dough on a lightly floured surface or stretch it onto a pizza stone or baking sheet.

3. Spread pizza sauce evenly over the dough, leaving a small border around the edges.

4. Sprinkle shredded mozzarella cheese over the sauce.

5. In a pan, heat olive oil over medium heat. Add minced garlic, and sliced mushrooms, and cook until mushrooms are tender. Season with salt and pepper.

6. Distribute the sautéed mushrooms evenly over the pizza.

7. Scatter fresh spinach leaves on top.

8. Optionally, sprinkle red pepper flakes for added spice.

9. Bake the pizza in the preheated oven according to the dough instructions or until the crust is golden and the cheese is melted and bubbly (usually around 12-15 minutes).

10. Once done, remove the pizza from the oven and let it cool for a few minutes.

11. Slice the pizza and serve hot.

Cauliflower Mac and Cheese Recipe

Servings: 4

45 minutes

Ingredients

- 2 cups elbow macaroni (or any pasta of choice)

- 1 small head of cauliflower, cut into florets

- 2 tablespoons butter

- 2 tablespoons all-purpose flour

- 2 cups milk (or plant-based milk)

- 2 cups shredded cheddar cheese

- 1/2 cup grated Parmesan cheese

- Salt and pepper to taste

- 1/2 cup breadcrumbs (optional, for topping)

- Fresh parsley, chopped (for garnish)

Tools

- Pot for boiling pasta

- Steamer basket or microwave-safe dish (for steaming cauliflower)

- Large saucepan

- Whisk

- Baking dish

Instructions

1. Preheat your oven to 350°F (175°C).

2. Cook the pasta according to package instructions until al dente. Drain and set aside.

3. Steam the cauliflower until tender, about 5-7 minutes. Alternatively, you can microwave the cauliflower with a bit of water for 4-5 minutes.

4. In a large saucepan, melt the butter over medium heat. Add the flour and whisk continuously for about 1-2 minutes to create a roux.

5. Gradually pour in the milk while whisking to avoid lumps. Continue whisking until the mixture thickens, about 5 minutes.

6. Reduce the heat to low. Add the shredded cheddar cheese and grated Parmesan cheese. Stir until the cheeses are fully melted and the sauce is smooth.

7. Season the cheese sauce with salt and pepper to taste.

8. Add the steamed cauliflower to the cheese sauce and stir until well coated.

9. Combine the cooked pasta with the cauliflower and cheese mixture.

Vegetarian Fried Rice Recipe

4 servings

25 minutes

Ingredients

- 2 cups cooked jasmine or basmati rice (preferably day-old and chilled)

- 2 tablespoons vegetable oil

- 1 cup mixed vegetables (peas, carrots, corn, diced bell peppers)

- 1/2 cup diced tofu or tempeh (optional)

- 2 cloves garlic, minced

- 2 green onions, sliced

- 2 tablespoons soy sauce

- 1 tablespoon oyster sauce (optional, for added flavor)

- 1 teaspoon sesame oil

- 1/2 teaspoon ground black pepper

- 2 eggs, lightly beaten

- Fresh cilantro or chopped green onions for garnish (optional)

Tools

- Wok or large skillet

- Spatula

- Cutting board

- Knife

Instructions

1. Cook the rice according to package instructions. For better results, use day-old rice that has been refrigerated.

   - Dice the tofu or tempeh (if using).

   - Prepare the mixed vegetables.

2. Heat vegetable oil in a wok or large skillet over medium-high heat.

3. Add minced garlic and diced tofu or tempeh to the pan. Stir-fry until tofu or tempeh is golden brown.

4. Add mixed vegetables to the pan and stir-fry for 2-3 minutes until they are tender-crisp.

5. Add the chilled cooked rice to the wok. Use a spatula to break up any clumps.

6. Drizzle soy sauce, oyster sauce (if using), and sesame oil over the rice. Sprinkle black pepper. Stir well to combine.

7. Push the rice mixture to one side of the pan, creating a space. Pour the beaten eggs into the space and scramble them until just cooked.

8. Mix the scrambled eggs into the rice and vegetable mixture. Stir everything together until well combined.

9. Add sliced green onions and toss the fried rice one last time.

10. Serve

Chickpea and Vegetable Stir Fry Recipe

Servings: 4

30 minutes

Ingredients

- 2 cans (15 oz each) chickpeas, drained and rinsed

- 2 cups mixed vegetables (bell peppers, broccoli, carrots, snap peas, etc.), chopped

- 1 cup cherry tomatoes, halved

- 1/2 cup red onion, thinly sliced

- 3 cloves garlic, minced

- 1-inch ginger, grated

- 1/4 cup soy sauce

- 2 tablespoons hoisin sauce

- 1 tablespoon sesame oil

- 1 tablespoon vegetable oil

- 1 tablespoon rice vinegar

- 1 teaspoon sriracha sauce (optional, for heat)

- Cooked brown rice or quinoa for serving

- Sesame seeds and chopped green onions for garnish

Tools

- Wok or large skillet

- Stirring utensil

- Cutting board

- Knife

Instructions

1. Drain and rinse the chickpeas. Prepare all the vegetables by chopping them into bite-sized pieces.

2. Heat vegetable oil and sesame oil in a wok or large skillet over medium-high heat.

3. Add minced garlic and grated ginger to the pan. Stir-fry for about 30 seconds until fragrant.

4. Add sliced red onion and mixed vegetables to the pan. Stir-fry for 3-4 minutes until the vegetables are slightly tender but still crisp.

5. Add chickpeas to the pan and continue stir-frying for an additional 2-3 minutes.

6. In a small bowl, mix soy sauce, hoisin sauce, rice vinegar, and sriracha (if using). Pour the sauce over the chickpeas and vegetables.

7. Add halved cherry tomatoes to the pan and stir-fry for another 2 minutes until they are heated through but not mushy.

8. Taste and adjust the seasoning, adding more soy sauce or other sauces if needed.

9. Serve the chickpea and vegetable stir fry over cooked brown rice or quinoa.

10. Garnish with sesame seeds and chopped green onions.

Easy Vegetarian Tacos Recipe

Servings: 4

25 minutes

Ingredients

For the Filling

- 1 can (15 oz) black beans, drained and rinsed

- 1 cup corn kernels (fresh, frozen, or canned)

- 1 bell pepper, diced

- 1 small red onion, finely chopped

- 1 teaspoon ground cumin

- 1 teaspoon chili powder

- Salt and pepper to taste

- 2 tablespoons olive oil

For the Toppings

- Shredded lettuce

- Diced tomatoes

- Salsa

- Guacamole or sliced avocado

- Shredded cheese (cheddar or Mexican blend)

- Fresh cilantro, chopped

- Lime wedges

For Assembling

- Soft taco shells or tortillas

Tools

- Skillet

- Wooden spoon

- Cutting board

- Knife

Instructions

1. Drain and rinse black beans and Dice bell pepper, chop red onion, and prepare other toppings.

2. In a skillet, heat olive oil over medium heat. Add diced bell pepper and chopped red onion. Sauté until vegetables are softened, about 3-4 minutes.

3. Add black beans and corn to the skillet. Stir in ground cumin, chili powder, salt, and pepper. Cook for an additional 5-6 minutes until everything is heated through.

4. Warm the taco shells or tortillas according to the package instructions.

5. Spoon the bean and corn mixture into each taco shell.6. Adding Toppings

   - Top with shredded lettuce, diced tomatoes, salsa, guacamole or avocado slices, shredded cheese, and chopped cilantro.

7. Serving

   - Serve with lime wedges on the side.

MILK FREE

Honey Cinnamon Bars Recipe

Servings: 12 bars

40 minutes

Ingredients

For the Bars

- 1 cup all-purpose flour

- 1 cup rolled oats

- 1/2 teaspoon baking soda

- 1/4 teaspoon salt

- 1/2 cup unsalted butter, softened

- 1/2 cup honey

- 1 teaspoon vanilla extract

For the Cinnamon Swirl

- 1/4 cup honey

- 2 teaspoons ground cinnamon

Tools

- 8x8-inch baking pan

- Parchment paper

- Mixing bowls

- Electric mixer or hand whisk

- Spatula

Instructions

1. Preheat your oven to 350°F (175°C). Grease and line an 8x8-inch baking pan with parchment paper, leaving an overhang on the sides for easy removal.

2. In a bowl, whisk together flour, rolled oats, baking soda, and salt. Set aside.

3. In a separate bowl, using an electric mixer or a hand whisk, cream together softened butter, honey, and vanilla extract until smooth and well combined.

4. Gradually add the dry ingredients to the wet ingredients, mixing until just combined. Do not overmix.

5. In a small bowl, mix honey and ground cinnamon to create the cinnamon swirl.

6. Spread about two-thirds of the oat mixture evenly into the prepared baking pan, pressing it down with a spatula.

7. Drizzle the cinnamon swirl mixture over the oat layer.

8. Crumble the remaining oat mixture over the cinnamon swirl layer, creating a crumbly topping.

9. Bake in the preheated oven for about 25 minutes or until the edges are golden brown.

10. Allow the bars to cool completely in the pan. Once cooled, lift the parchment paper overhang to easily remove the bars. Slice into squares or bars.

Creamy Garlic and Mushroom Pasta (Dairy-Free)

Servings: 4

30 minutes

Ingredients

- 8 oz (about 225g) pasta of your choice

- 2 tablespoons olive oil

- 1 pound (about 450g) mushrooms, sliced

- 4 cloves garlic, minced

- 1 can (14 oz) coconut milk (full-fat for creaminess)

- 2 tablespoons nutritional yeast (optional, for a cheesy flavor)

- Salt and pepper to taste

- Fresh parsley, chopped, for garnish

- Red pepper flakes (optional, for added spice)

Tools

- Large pot for boiling pasta

- Skillet

- Wooden spoon

- Cooking pot Instructions

Ingridients

1. Cook Pasta

- Cook the pasta according to package instructions in a large pot of salted boiling water. Drain and set aside.

2. Sauté Mushrooms and Garlic

- In a skillet, heat olive oil over medium heat. Add sliced mushrooms and sauté until they release their moisture and become golden brown, about 5-7 minutes. Add minced garlic and cook for an additional 1-2 minutes.

3. Prepare Creamy Sauce

- Pour in the coconut milk and bring the mixture to a gentle simmer. Stir in nutritional yeast (if using), salt, and pepper. Let it simmer for another 5-7 minutes, allowing the flavors to meld and the sauce to thicken slightly.

4. Combine Pasta and Sauce

- Add the cooked and drained pasta to the skillet with the creamy mushroom sauce. Toss everything together until the pasta is well coated.

5. Adjust Seasoning

- Taste and adjust the seasoning as needed, adding more salt and pepper if necessary.

6. Serve

- Serve the creamy garlic and mushroom pasta hot, garnished with chopped fresh parsley and red pepper flakes if desired.

Coconut Pudding Recipe Without Milk

Servings: 4

2 hours

Ingredients

- 1 can (13.5 oz) coconut milk (full-fat for creamier pudding)

- 1/3 cup cornstarch

- 1/2 cup granulated sugar

- 1/4 teaspoon salt

- 1 teaspoon vanilla extract

- Shredded coconut for garnish (optional)

- Fresh berries for topping (optional)

Tools

- Saucepan

- Whisk

- Mixing bowl

- Serving glasses or bowls

Instructions

1. Mix Dry Ingredients

   - In a mixing bowl, combine cornstarch, sugar, and salt. Whisk until well mixed.

2. Heat Coconut Milk

   - In a saucepan, pour the coconut milk. Heat it over medium heat until it's warm but not boiling.

3. Combine Ingredients

   - Gradually whisk the dry ingredients into the warm coconut milk, ensuring there are no lumps.

4. Cooking Pudding

   - Continue to cook over medium heat, whisking constantly, until the mixture thickens to a pudding-like consistency. This usually takes about 5-7 minutes.

5. Add Vanilla Extract

   - Once thickened, remove the saucepan from heat. Stir in the vanilla extract.

6. Cool and Chill

   - Allow the coconut pudding to cool for a few minutes before transferring it to serving glasses or bowls. Cover and refrigerate for at least 2 hours to set.

7. Serve

   - Garnish with shredded coconut and top with fresh berries if desired.

8. Enjoy

   - Serve and enjoy your dairy-free Coconut Pudding!

Veggie Pinwheels Recipe

Servings: 4-6

25 minutes

Ingredients

For the Veggie Filling

- 1 cup hummus (store-bought or homemade)

- 1 large carrot, julienned or shredded

- 1 bell pepper (any color), thinly sliced

- 1 cucumber, thinly sliced

- 1/2 cup baby spinach leaves, chopped

- Salt and pepper to taste

For the Wraps

- 4 large flour tortillas or whole wheat wraps

Tools

- Spatula or butter knife

- Cutting board

- Sharp knife

Instructions

1. Prepare Ingredients

   - Wash and prepare all the vegetables. Julienne or shred the carrot, thinly slice the bell pepper and cucumber, and chop the baby spinach.

2. Spread Hummus

   - Lay out the tortillas on a clean surface. Spread an even layer of hummus over each tortilla, leaving a small border around the edges.

3. Layer Vegetables

   - Sprinkle the julienned or shredded carrots, sliced bell pepper, cucumber, and chopped baby spinach evenly over the hummus.

4. Season and Roll

   - Season the vegetables with salt and pepper to taste. Starting from one edge, tightly roll up each tortilla into a log or cylinder.

5. Chill and Slice

   - Wrap the rolled tortillas in plastic wrap and refrigerate for at least 30 minutes to firm up. This makes slicing easier.

6. Slice into Pinwheels

   - Once chilled, use a sharp knife to slice each rolled tortilla into 1-inch pinwheels.

7. Serve- Arrange the veggie pinwheels on a serving platter and serve chilled.

Dairy-Free Chocolate Chia Pudding Recipe

Servings: 2

5 minutes prep- 2hrs chilling time

Ingredients

- 1/4 cup chia seeds

- 1 cup almond milk (or any other non-dairy milk)

- 2 tablespoons cocoa powder

- 2-3 tablespoons maple syrup or agave nectar (adjust to taste)

- 1/2 teaspoon vanilla extract

- A pinch of salt

- Optional toppings: Fresh berries, sliced bananas, shredded coconut, or chopped nuts

Tools

- Mixing bowl

- Whisk

- Jars or bowls for serving

Instructions

1. Mix Ingredients

- In a mixing bowl, combine chia seeds, almond milk, cocoa powder, maple syrup, vanilla extract, and a pinch of salt.

2. Whisk Thoroughly

- Whisk the mixture thoroughly to ensure the chia seeds are evenly distributed and not clumped together.

3. Refrigerate

- Cover the bowl and refrigerate for at least 2 hours or overnight. This allows the chia seeds to absorb the liquid and create a pudding-like consistency.

4. Stir Again

- After the initial refrigeration, give the mixture a good stir. If it seems too thick, you can add a bit more almond milk to reach your desired consistency.

5. Serve

- Spoon the chocolate chia pudding into serving jars or bowls.

6. Top with Toppings

- Add your favorite toppings like fresh berries, sliced bananas, shredded coconut, or chopped nuts.

Serve chilled and enjoy your delicious and dairy-free chocolate chia pudding!

Avocado Toast with Tomato and Basil

Servings: 2

5 minutes

Ingredients

- 2 slices of whole-grain bread (or bread of your choice)

- 1 ripe avocado

- 1 medium-sized tomato, sliced

- Fresh basil leaves

- Olive oil

- Salt and pepper to taste

- Optional toppings: Red pepper flakes, balsamic glaze, or a squeeze of lemon juice

Tools

- Toaster or toaster oven

- Cutting board

- Knife

- Fork for mashing

Instructions

1. Toast the Bread

   - Toast the slices of bread to your preferred level of crispiness.

2. Prepare the Avocado

   - While the bread is toasting, cut the avocado in half and remove the pit. Scoop the avocado flesh into a bowl.

3. Mash the Avocado

   - Using a fork, mash the avocado until you achieve your desired level of smoothness or chunkiness.

4. Season the Avocado

   - Season the mashed avocado with salt and pepper to taste. Mix well.

5. Assemble the Toast

   - Spread the mashed avocado evenly onto each slice of toasted bread.

6. Add Tomato Slices

   - Place tomato slices on top of the mashed avocado.

7. Garnish with Basil

   - Tear fresh basil leaves and scatter them over the tomato slices.

8. Drizzle with Olive Oil

   - Drizzle a bit of olive oil over the top of each avocado toast.

Vegan Chocolate Banana Ice Cream Recipe

Servings: 2

2-3 hours total

Ingredients

- 3 ripe bananas, sliced and frozen

- 2 tablespoons cocoa powder

- 1-2 tablespoons maple syrup or agave nectar (adjust to taste)

- 1/2 teaspoon vanilla extract

- Optional toppings: Vegan chocolate chips, sliced strawberries, or chopped nuts

Tools

- Food processor or blender

- Silicone spatula or spoon

Instructions

1. Freeze Bananas

   - Peel and slice ripe bananas into rounds. Place the banana slices on a tray or in a bag and freeze for at least 2-3 hours or overnight.

2. Blend Frozen Bananas

   - Once the bananas are frozen, place them in a food processor or blender.

3. Add Cocoa Powder and Sweetener

   - Add cocoa powder, maple syrup (or agave nectar), and vanilla extract to the frozen banana slices.

4. Blend Until Smooth

   - Blend the mixture until it becomes smooth and creamy. You may need to pause and scrape down the sides with a spatula to ensure even blending.

5. Check Consistency

   - Taste the ice cream base and adjust sweetness or cocoa powder if needed.

6. Optional Toppings

   - If desired, fold in vegan chocolate chips or add toppings like sliced strawberries or chopped nuts.

7. Serve Immediately or Freeze for a Firmer Texture

   - For a soft-serve consistency, serve the chocolate banana ice cream immediately. If you prefer a firmer texture, transfer the mixture to a container and freeze for an additional 1-2 hours.

8. Scoop and Enjoy

   - Scoop the vegan chocolate banana ice cream into bowls or cones. Add more toppings if desired.

FISH FREE

Vegan Lentil and Vegetable Soup

 Servings: 4

 45 minutes

Ingredients

- 1 cup dry lentils, rinsed

- 1 onion, diced

- 2 carrots, diced

- 2 celery stalks, diced

- 3 cloves garlic, minced

- 1 can (14 oz) diced tomatoes

- 6 cups vegetable broth

- 1 teaspoon ground cumin

- 1 teaspoon dried thyme

- 1 teaspoon paprika

- Salt and pepper to taste

- 2 tablespoons olive oil

- Fresh parsley for garnish (optional)

Tools

- Large pot

- Wooden spoon

- Cutting board

- Knife

- Can opener

- Measuring cups and spoons

Instructions

1. Prepare Vegetables

  - Dice the onion, carrots, and celery. Mince the garlic.

2. Sauté Vegetables

  - In a large pot, heat olive oil over medium heat. Add diced onion, carrots, celery, and minced garlic. Sauté until vegetables are softened, about 5-7 minutes.

3. Add Lentils and Spices

  - Add rinsed lentils to the pot. Stir in ground cumin, dried thyme, paprika, salt, and pepper.

4. Pour in Tomatoes and Broth

  - Pour in the diced tomatoes (with their juice) and vegetable broth. Bring the mixture to a boil.

5. Simmer

  - Reduce the heat to low, cover the pot, and simmer for about 20-25 minutes or until the lentils are tender.

6. Adjust Seasoning

  - Taste the soup and adjust the seasoning if needed. Add more salt and pepper to suit your taste.

7. Serve

Vegetable Sushi Rolls

Servings 3

45 minutes

Ingredients:

- 2 cups sushi rice, cooked and seasoned with rice vinegar

- 4 sheets of nori (seaweed)

- 1 cucumber, julienned

- 1 carrot, julienned

- 1 avocado, sliced

- Soy sauce, for dipping

- Pickled ginger, for serving

- Wasabi (optional)

- Sesame seeds for garnish (optional)

Tools:

- Bamboo sushi rolling mat

- Plastic wrap

- Sharp knife

Instructions:

1. Prepare Ingredients

   - Cook sushi rice according to package instructions. Season with rice vinegar and let it cool.

2. Prep Vegetables

   - Julienne cucumber, carrot, and slice the avocado.

3. Assemble Sushi Rolls

   - Place a sheet of nori on the bamboo sushi rolling mat, shiny side down. Moisten your hands to prevent the rice from sticking and spread a thin layer of rice over the nori, leaving a small border at the top.

4. Add Vegetables

   - Place julienned cucumber, carrot, and avocado slices along the bottom edge of the rice.

5. Roll the Sushi

   - Using the bamboo mat, tightly roll the nori and rice over the vegetables. Seal the edge with a bit of water.

6. Slice the Roll

   - Using a sharp knife, moistened with water, slice the roll into bite-sized pieces.

7. Repeat

   - Repeat the process with the remaining nori sheets and ingredients.

8. Serve

   - Arrange the sushi rolls on a plate, along with pickled ginger. Optionally, sprinkle sesame seeds on top for garnish.

   - Serve with soy sauce for dipping. Add wasabi if desired.

Quinoa Patties Recipe for Kids

Servings: 4

30 minutes

Ingredients

- 1 cup cooked quinoa, cooled

- 1/2 cup breadcrumbs

- 1/4 cup grated cheese (cheddar or Parmesan)

- 1/4 cup finely chopped onion

- 1/4 cup finely chopped bell pepper (any color)

- 1/4 cup finely chopped carrots

- 2 cloves garlic, minced

- 2 tablespoons chopped fresh parsley

- 2 large eggs

- 1 teaspoon dried oregano

- Salt and pepper to taste

- Cooking oil for pan-frying

Tools

- Mixing bowl

- Frying pan

- Spatula

- Plate lined with paper towels

Instructions

1. Prepare Quinoa

   - Cook quinoa according to package instructions. Allow it to cool to room temperature.

2. Mix Ingredients

   - In a mixing bowl, combine cooked quinoa, breadcrumbs, grated cheese, chopped onion, bell pepper, carrots, garlic, parsley, eggs, oregano, salt, and pepper. Mix well until all ingredients are evenly combined.

3. Form Patties

   - Take a small portion of the mixture and shape it into a patty. The mixture should hold together well. If it's too wet, add a bit more breadcrumbs.

4. Heat Oil

   - Heat cooking oil in a frying pan over medium heat.

5. Pan-Fry Patties

   - Place the quinoa patties in the hot pan and cook for about 3-4 minutes on each side or until golden brown and crispy. Cook in batches to avoid overcrowding the pan.

6. Drain Excess Oil

   - Once cooked, transfer the patties to a plate lined with paper towels to absorb any excess oil.

7. Serve

Lemon Garlic Butter Baked Tofu for Kids

Servings: 4

1 hour 10 minutes

Ingredients

- 1 block extra-firm tofu, pressed and cut into cubes

- 3 tablespoons unsalted vegan butter, melted

- 2 tablespoons soy sauce or tamari

- 2 tablespoons lemon juice

- 2 cloves garlic, minced

- 1 teaspoon dried thyme (optional)

- Salt and pepper to taste

- Fresh parsley, chopped, for garnish

Tools

- Baking sheet

- Parchment paper

- Mixing bowl

Instructions

1. Press Tofu

   - Press the tofu to remove excess water. You can use a tofu press or wrap the tofu block in a clean kitchen towel and place a heavy object on top for 15-30 minutes.

2. Preheat Oven

   - Preheat the oven to 375°F (190°C). Line a baking sheet with parchment paper.

3. Prepare Marinade

   - In a mixing bowl, whisk together melted vegan butter, soy sauce, lemon juice, minced garlic, dried thyme (if using), salt, and pepper.

4. Marinate Tofu

   - Cut the pressed tofu into cubes and gently toss them in the marinade, ensuring they are well coated. Allow the tofu to marinate for at least 30 minutes in the refrigerator.

5. Bake Tofu

   - Spread the marinated tofu cubes evenly on the prepared baking sheet. Bake in the preheated oven for about 25 minutes or until the edges are golden brown and crispy, flipping the tofu halfway through.

6. Garnish and Serve

   - Remove the baked tofu from the oven, garnish with chopped fresh parsley, and serve warm.

Cauliflower Buffalo Bites

Servings: 4

40 minutes

Ingredients

- 1 large cauliflower head, cut into florets

- 1 cup all-purpose flour (or chickpea flour for a gluten-free option)

- 1 cup plant-based milk (almond, soy, or oat)

- 1 teaspoon garlic powder

- 1 teaspoon onion powder

- 1 teaspoon smoked paprika

- 1/2 teaspoon salt

- 1/4 teaspoon black pepper

- 1 cup breadcrumbs (or panko breadcrumbs)

- 1 cup buffalo sauce

- 2 tablespoons vegan butter, melted

- Green onions and vegan ranch dressing for garnish (optional)

Tools

- Baking sheet

- Parchment paper

- Mixing bowls

- Whisk

- Tongs

Instructions

1. Preheat Oven

   - Preheat the oven to 450°F (230°C). Line a baking sheet with parchment paper.

2. Prepare Batter

   - In a bowl, whisk together the flour, plant-based milk, garlic powder, onion powder, smoked paprika, salt, and black pepper until smooth.

3. Coat Cauliflower

   - Dip each cauliflower floret into the batter, allowing excess batter to drip off.

4. Breadcrumb Coating

   - Roll the battered cauliflower in breadcrumbs until evenly coated.

5. Bake

   - Place the coated cauliflower on the prepared baking sheet. Bake for 20-25 minutes or until golden brown and crispy.

6. Prepare Buffalo Sauce

   - While the cauliflower is baking, mix buffalo sauce and melted vegan butter in a bowl.

7. Toss in Buffalo Sauce

   - Once the cauliflower is done baking, transfer it to a large bowl. Pour the buffalo sauce mixture over the cauliflower and toss until evenly coated.

Stuffed Acorn Squash Recipe for Kids

Servings: 4

1 hour

Ingredients

- 2 acorn squashes, halved and seeds removed

- 1 cup quinoa, cooked

- 1 can (15 oz) black beans, drained and rinsed

- 1 cup corn kernels (fresh, frozen, or canned)

- 1 cup diced tomatoes

- 1/2 cup diced red bell pepper

- 1/2 cup diced green bell pepper

- 1/4 cup chopped fresh cilantro

- 2 tablespoons olive oil

- 1 teaspoon ground cumin

- 1 teaspoon chili powder

- 1/2 teaspoon garlic powder

- Salt and pepper to taste

- Optional toppings: Avocado slices, vegan cheese, salsa

Tools

- Baking sheet

- Mixing bowl

- Spoon

Instructions

1. Preheat Oven

   - Preheat the oven to 375°F (190°C).

2. Prepare Acorn Squash

   - Cut the acorn squashes in half and scoop out the seeds. Place them on a baking sheet, cut side up.

3. Roast Acorn Squash

   - Drizzle olive oil over the acorn squashes and sprinkle with salt and pepper. Roast in the preheated oven for about 30-40 minutes or until the squash is fork-tender.

4. Prepare Quinoa Mixture

   - In a mixing bowl, combine cooked quinoa, black beans, corn, diced tomatoes, red bell pepper, green bell pepper, cilantro, ground cumin, chili powder, garlic powder, salt, and pepper. Mix well.

5. Stuff Acorn Squash

   - Once the acorn squashes are roasted, fill each squash half with the quinoa mixture.

6. Bake Again

   - Place the stuffed acorn squashes back in the oven for an additional 15 minutes or until the filling is heated through.

Vegan Sloppy Joes for Kids

Servings: 4

30 minutes

Ingredients

- 1 tablespoon olive oil

- 1 onion, finely chopped

- 1 bell pepper, finely chopped (any color)

- 2 cloves garlic, minced

- 1 can (15 oz) lentils, drained and rinsed (or cooked green or brown lentils)

- 1 can (15 oz) crushed tomatoes

- 2 tablespoons tomato paste

- 2 tablespoons soy sauce or tamari

- 1 tablespoon maple syrup or agave nectar

- 1 teaspoon chili powder

- 1/2 teaspoon smoked paprika

- 1/2 teaspoon ground cumin

- Salt and pepper to taste

- Hamburger buns or rolls

- Optional toppings: Pickles, vegan cheese, lettuce

Tools

- Skillet

- Wooden spoon

Instructions

1. Sauté Vegetables

   - Heat olive oil in a skillet over medium heat. Add chopped onion and bell pepper. Sauté until softened, about 5 minutes.

2. Add Garlic and Lentils

   - Add minced garlic and lentils to the skillet. Stir and cook for an additional 2 minutes.

3. Combine Sauce Ingredients

   - In a small bowl, whisk together crushed tomatoes, tomato paste, soy sauce, maple syrup, chili powder, smoked paprika, ground cumin, salt, and pepper.

4. Simmer Sauce

   - Pour the sauce mixture over the lentil and vegetable mixture in the skillet. Stir to combine. Simmer for 10-15 minutes, allowing the flavors to meld and the mixture to thicken.

5. Adjust Seasoning

   - Taste and adjust seasoning if needed. Add more salt, pepper, or spices according to your preference.

6. Toast Hamburger Buns

   - While the mixture is simmering, lightly toast the hamburger buns or rolls.

7. Assemble Sloppy Joes and Enjoy!

Veggie Stir-Fried Noodles

Servings: 4

30 minutes

Ingredients

- 8 oz (about 225g) stir-fry noodles (rice or wheat noodles)

- 2 tablespoons vegetable oil

- 1 onion, thinly sliced

- 2 carrots, julienned

- 1 bell pepper, thinly sliced (any color)

- 1 zucchini, julienned

- 2 cups broccoli florets

- 3 cloves garlic, minced

- 1-inch piece of ginger, grated

- 1/4 cup soy sauce

- 2 tablespoons hoisin sauce

- 1 tablespoon sesame oil

- 1 tablespoon rice vinegar

- 1 tablespoon maple syrup or agave nectar

- Sesame seeds and chopped green onions for garnish (optional)

Tools

- Wok or large skillet

- Pot for boiling noodles

- Wooden spoon or spatula

Instructions

1. Cook Noodles

   - Cook the stir-fry noodles according to the package instructions. Drain and set aside.

2. Prepare Sauce

   - In a small bowl, whisk together soy sauce, hoisin sauce, sesame oil, rice vinegar, and maple syrup. Set aside.

3. Stir-Fry Vegetables

   - Heat vegetable oil in a wok or large skillet over medium-high heat. Add sliced onion, julienned carrots, sliced bell pepper, julienned zucchini, and broccoli florets. Stir-fry for 3-5 minutes or until the vegetables are slightly tender but still crisp.

4. Add Garlic and Ginger

   - Add minced garlic and grated ginger to the vegetables. Stir-fry for an additional 1-2 minutes until fragrant.

5. Combine Noodles and Sauce

   - Add the cooked noodles to the wok or skillet. Pour the sauce over the noodles and vegetables. Toss everything together to ensure the noodles are well coated in the sauce.

6. Finish Cooking by stir frying for 2-3 minutes...

Tofu Rice Bowls

Servings: 4

35 minutes

Ingredients

- 1 cup uncooked jasmine rice (or rice of your choice)

- 1 block extra-firm tofu, pressed and cubed

- 2 tablespoons soy sauce or tamari

- 1 tablespoon sesame oil

- 1 tablespoon rice vinegar

- 1 tablespoon maple syrup or agave nectar

- 1 tablespoon cornstarch

- 2 tablespoons vegetable oil (for frying tofu)

- 4 cups mixed vegetables (broccoli, bell peppers, carrots, snap peas, etc.)

- 2 cloves garlic, minced

- 1 teaspoon fresh ginger, grated

- Sesame seeds and sliced green onions for garnish

- Optional: Sriracha or your favorite hot sauce

Tools

- Saucepan for rice

- Skillet or wok

- Mixing bowl

- Tongs or spatula

Instructions

1. Cook Rice

   - Cook the jasmine rice according to package instructions.

2. Prepare Tofu

   - Press the tofu to remove excess water. Cut into cubes. In a mixing bowl, whisk together soy sauce, sesame oil, rice vinegar, maple syrup, and cornstarch. Add tofu cubes to the bowl and gently toss until coated.

3. Fry Tofu

   - Heat vegetable oil in a skillet over medium-high heat. Add the tofu cubes and fry until golden brown on all sides. Remove tofu from the skillet and set aside.

4. Stir-Fry Vegetables

   - In the same skillet, add a bit more oil if needed. Stir-fry the mixed vegetables, garlic, and ginger until the vegetables are tender-crisp.

5. Combine Tofu and Vegetables

   - Return the fried tofu to the skillet with the vegetables. Toss everything together to combine and heat through.

6. Assemble Rice Bowls

   - Divide the cooked rice among four bowls. Top with the tofu and vegetable mixture.

NUTS FREE

NUT FREE

Vanilla Pudding Parfait

Servings: 4

15 minutes preparation and 1 hour chilling

Ingredients

- 1 package (3.4 oz) vanilla pudding mix (instant or cook-and-serve)

- 2 cups cold non-dairy milk (such as almond, soy, or oat milk)

- 1 teaspoon vanilla extract

- 1 cup crushed graham crackers

- 2 ripe bananas, sliced

- Whipped coconut cream or non-dairy whipped topping

- Fresh berries for garnish (optional)

Tools

- Mixing bowl

- Whisk

- Serving glasses or bowls

Instructions

1. Prepare Vanilla Pudding

   - In a mixing bowl, combine the vanilla pudding mix with cold non-dairy milk. Add vanilla extract. Whisk until smooth and well combined. If using cook-and-serve pudding, follow the package instructions to cook and cool it.

2. Chill Pudding (if needed)

   - If using instant pudding, chill the mixture in the refrigerator for about 1 hour or as per the package instructions until it thickens.

3. Assemble Parfait

   - In serving glasses or bowls, create layers starting with a spoonful of crushed graham crackers at the bottom.

4. Add Pudding Layer

   - Spoon a layer of the chilled vanilla pudding over the graham crackers.

5. Layer Sliced Bananas

   - Add a layer of sliced bananas over the pudding.

6. Repeat Layers

   - Repeat the process by adding another layer of graham crackers, pudding, and sliced bananas until you reach the top of the glass.

7. Top with Whipped Coconut Cream

   - Finish the parfait by topping it with a generous dollop of whipped coconut cream or non-dairy whipped topping.

8. Garnish (Optional)

   - Garnish with fresh berries or additional crushed graham crackers if desired.

Simple Vegetarian Chili for Kids

Servings: 4-6

35 minutes

Ingredients

- 2 cans (15 oz each) mixed beans (black, kidney, or pinto), drained and rinsed

- 1 can (15 oz) diced tomatoes

- 1 cup corn kernels (fresh, frozen, or canned)

- 1 onion, finely chopped

- 1 bell pepper, diced (any color)

- 2 cloves garlic, minced

- 2 tablespoons chili powder

- 1 teaspoon ground cumin

- 4 cups vegetable broth

- Salt and pepper to taste

- Optional toppings: Shredded cheese, diced avocado, chopped green onions

Tools

- Large pot

- Wooden spoon

Instructions

1. Saute Vegetables

- In a large pot over medium heat, sauté chopped onions, diced bell peppers, and minced garlic until softened, about 5 minutes.

2. Add Beans and Corn

- Add mixed beans, diced tomatoes, and corn to the pot. Stir to combine.

3. Seasoning

- Sprinkle chili powder and ground cumin over the ingredients. Stir well to coat.

4. Pour in Vegetable Broth

- Pour vegetable broth into the pot. Season with salt and pepper to taste.

5. Simmer

- Bring the chili to a boil, then reduce the heat to low. Cover and let it simmer for about 15-20 minutes.

6. Adjust Seasoning

- Taste and adjust the seasoning if needed. Add more chili powder or salt as desired.

7. Serve

- Ladle the simple vegetarian chili into bowls. Top with shredded cheese, diced avocado, or chopped green onions if desired.

Rainbow Rice Bowls

Servings: 4

30 minutes

Ingredients

- 2 cups white rice, cooked

- 1 red bell pepper, diced

- 1 yellow bell pepper, diced

- 1 orange bell pepper, diced

- 1 cucumber, diced

- 1 cup cherry tomatoes, halved

- 1 cup corn kernels (fresh, frozen, or canned)

- 1 avocado, sliced

- 1 cup black beans, drained and rinsed

- 1/4 cup fresh cilantro, chopped (optional)

- 1 lime, cut into wedges

- Salt and pepper to taste

Tools

- Mixing bowls

- Wooden spoon or spatula

Instructions

1. Cook Rice

- If not using pre-cooked rice, cook the white rice according to package instructions.

2. Prepare Ingredients

- While the rice is cooking, prepare the vegetables and other ingredients by washing, chopping, and slicing them as needed.

3. Assemble Bowls

- In individual bowls, arrange the cooked rice as the base.

4. Create Rainbow Layers

- On top of the rice, create rainbow layers by adding diced red, yellow, and orange bell peppers, cucumber, cherry tomatoes, corn, avocado slices, and black beans.

5. Garnish

- Sprinkle fresh cilantro over the top for added flavor (optional).

6. Season and Squeeze Lime

- Season the rainbow rice bowls with salt and pepper to taste. Squeeze lime wedges over the bowls for a burst of citrus flavor.

7. Mix and Enjoy - Encourage kids to use a spoon or fork to mix the ingredients in their rainbow rice bowls before enjoying the colorful and tasty dish.

Banana Oat Muffins

Servings 3

30 minutes

Ingredients

- 2 ripe bananas, mashed

- 1 cup gluten-free rolled oats

- 1/2 cup milk (dairy or dairy-free alternative)

- 1/4 cup maple syrup or honey

- 1 teaspoon baking powder

- 1/2 teaspoon cinnamon

- 1/4 teaspoon salt

- Optional: Chocolate chips, raisins, or chopped nuts for added flavor

Tools

- Mixing bowl

- Muffin tin

- Cupcake liners (optional)

- Fork or potato masher

- Spoon or ice cream scoop

Instructions

1. Preheat Oven

   - Preheat your oven to 350°F (175°C). Line a muffin tin with cupcake liners or grease the muffin cups.

2. Mash Bananas

   - In a mixing bowl, mash the ripe bananas using a fork or potato masher until smooth.

3. Add Wet Ingredients

   - Add milk and maple syrup (or honey) to the mashed bananas. Mix well.

4. Add Dry Ingredients

   - Add gluten-free rolled oats, baking powder, cinnamon, and salt to the wet ingredients. Stir until just combined.

5. Optional Additions

   - If desired, fold in chocolate chips, raisins, or chopped nuts into the batter for added texture and flavor.

6. Fill Muffin Cups

   - Spoon the batter into the prepared muffin cups, filling each about 2/3 full.

7. Bake

   - Bake in the preheated oven for 15-20 minutes or until a toothpick inserted into the center of a muffin comes out clean.

Nut-Free Fruit Salad

Servings 4

15 minutes

Ingredients

- 2 cups strawberries, hulled and halved

- 1 cup blueberries

- 1 cup grapes, halved

- 2 kiwis, peeled and sliced

- 1 cup pineapple chunks

- 1 cup mango chunks

- 1 kiwi

- Fresh mint leaves for garnish (optional)

Optional Honey-Lime Dressing

- 2 tablespoons honey

- 1 tablespoon lime juice

Tools

- Cutting board and knife

- Mixing bowl

- Whisk

Instructions

1. Prepare the Fruits

 - Wash and prepare all the fruits as needed. Cut them into kid-friendly, bite-sized pieces.

2. Combine Fruits

 - In a large mixing bowl, combine the strawberries, blueberries, grapes, kiwis, pineapple, mango, and banana.

3. Optional Dressing

 - In a small bowl, whisk together honey and lime juice to create a simple dressing.

4. Drizzle Dressing

 - If using, drizzle the honey-lime dressing over the fruit salad. Gently toss to coat the fruits evenly.

5. Garnish

 - Garnish with fresh mint leaves for a burst of color and added freshness.

6. Chill (Optional)

 - If time allows, refrigerate the fruit salad for about 30 minutes before serving to enhance the flavors.

7. Serve

 - Serve the nut-free fruit salad in individual bowls or cups.

Nut-Free Banana Ice Cream

Servings: 3 cups

5 minutes preparation and more 2-3 hours

Ingredients

- Ripe bananas, sliced and frozen

- 1-2 tablespoons cocoa powder (nut-free)

- Toppings: sprinkles, sliced strawberries, or shredded coconut (optional)

Time

- Preparation Time 5 minutes

- Freezing Time 2-3 hours

- Total Time 2-3 hours and 5 minutes

Tools

- Food processor or blender

- Freezer-safe container

- Spoon or ice cream scoop

Servings

- This recipe makes approximately 2 servings.

Instructions

1. Slice and Freeze Bananas

   - Peel ripe bananas, slice them, and place the slices on a parchment-lined tray.

   - Freeze the banana slices for at least 2-3 hours or until solid.

2. Blend Frozen Bananas

   - Place the frozen banana slices in a food processor or blender.

   - Blend until the bananas become creamy and smooth. You may need to stop and scrape down the sides occasionally.

3. Add Cocoa Powder

   - Add 1-2 tablespoons of nut-free cocoa powder to the blended bananas.

   - Blend again until the cocoa powder is fully incorporated.

4. Adjust Consistency (Optional)

   - If the ice cream is too soft, you can transfer it to a freezer-safe container and freeze for an additional 30-60 minutes to firm it up.

5. Serve

   - Scoop the banana ice cream into bowls or cones.

Nut-Free Rice Krispie Treats

Servings: 12 treats

1 hour

Ingredients

- 6 cups gluten-free Rice Krispies cereal

- 1/4 cup unsalted butter or dairy-free alternative

- 1 package (about 10 ounces) marshmallows

Tools

- Large pot

- Wooden spoon or spatula

- 9x13 inch baking dish

- Cooking spray or extra butter for greasing

Instructions

1. Prepare Baking Dish

   - Grease a 9x13-inch baking dish with cooking spray or butter.

2. Melt Butter and Marshmallows

   - In a large pot, melt the butter over low heat.

   - Add the marshmallows and stir continuously until completely melted and smooth.

3. Mix in Rice Krispies

   - Remove the pot from heat and gently stir in the gluten-free Rice Krispies cereal until they are evenly coated with the marshmallow mixture.

4. Press into Baking Dish

   - Transfer the mixture to the prepared baking dish.

   - Using a buttered spatula or your hands (lightly greased), press the mixture evenly into the dish.

5. Cool and Cut

   - Allow the Rice Krispie Treats to cool at room temperature for at least 1 hour or until set.

   - Once cooled, cut into squares using a sharp knife.

6. Serve

   - Serve the nut-free Rice Krispie Treats and enjoy!

Feel free to get creative by adding gluten-free chocolate chips, sprinkles, or other kid-friendly toppings while the mixture is still warm for an extra touch of fun. These treats are perfect for lunchboxes, parties, or a sweet snack.

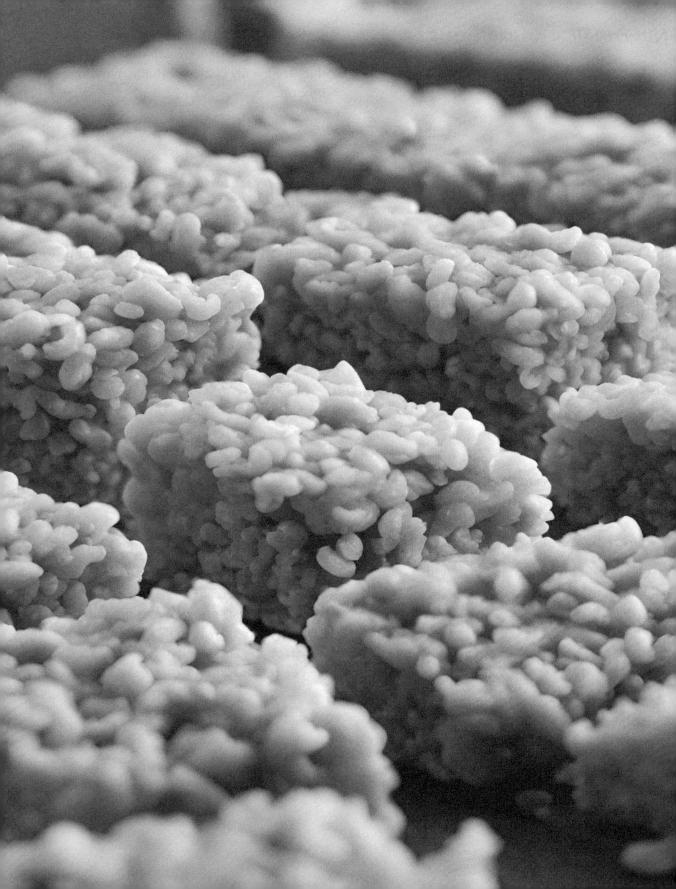

Fruit Popsicles

 6 popsicles

 4-6 hours

Ingredients

- Assorted fresh fruits (berries, kiwi, mango, etc.)

- Fruit juice (100% pure, no added sugar)

Tools

- Popsicle molds

- Popsicle sticks

Instructions

1. Prepare Fresh Fruits

   - Wash and cut assorted fresh fruits into small, bite-sized pieces.

2. Fill Popsicle Molds

   - Place the fruit pieces into the popsicle molds, distributing them evenly among the molds.

3. Pour Fruit Juice

   - Pour 100% pure fruit juice into the molds to cover the fruit pieces. Leave a small space at the top to allow for expansion during freezing.

4. Insert Popsicle Sticks

   - Insert popsicle sticks into the molds. Ensure they are centered in the liquid.

5. Freeze

   - Place the popsicle molds in the freezer and let them freeze for 4-6 hours or overnight until completely solid.

6. Unmold Popsicles

   - Once the popsicles are fully frozen, remove the molds from the freezer.

   - Run the molds briefly under warm water to help release the popsicles.

7. Serve and Enjoy

   - Serve the fruit popsicles immediately and enjoy this refreshing treat!

Fruit Salsa with Cinnamon Chips

3 servings

30 minutes

Ingredients

For Fruit Salsa:

- 2 cups assorted fruits (berries, kiwi, mango, etc.), finely diced

- 1 tablespoon sugar (adjust based on the sweetness of fruits)

- 1 teaspoon fresh lime or lemon juice

For Cinnamon Chips:

- 8 gluten-free tortillas

- 1/4 cup unsalted butter, melted (or dairy-free alternative)

- 1/4 cup granulated sugar

- 1 teaspoon ground cinnamon

Tools

- Mixing bowls

- Sharp knife and cutting board

- Baking sheets

- Pastry brush or spoon for applying butter

- Pizza cutter or knife

Servings

- This recipe makes approximately 4 servings.

Instructions

1. Preheat Oven

  - Preheat the oven to 350°F (175°C).

2. Prepare Fruit Salsa

  - Wash and finely dice the assorted fruits.

  - In a mixing bowl, combine the diced fruits, sugar, and lime or lemon juice. Toss gently to coat. Refrigerate while preparing cinnamon chips.

3. Make Cinnamon Sugar Mixture

  - In a small bowl, mix granulated sugar and ground cinnamon to coat the chips.

4. Prepare Cinnamon Chips

  - Brush each gluten-free tortilla with melted butter on both sides.

  - Sprinkle the cinnamon sugar mixture over each side of the tortillas, ensuring they are evenly coated.

  - Stack the tortillas and cut them into wedges using a pizza cutter or knife.

5. Bake Cinnamon Chips

  - Arrange the cinnamon-coated tortilla wedges on a baking sheet.

  - Bake in the preheated oven for 10-12 minutes or until the chips are crisp and golden.

WHEAT FREE

Zucchini Noodles with Pesto

Servings 2

30 minutes

Ingredients

- 4 medium-sized zucchini

- 1 cup cherry tomatoes, halved

- 1/2 cup pesto sauce (ensure it's gluten-free)

- 1/4 cup grated Parmesan cheese (optional)

- Salt and pepper to taste

- Olive oil for cooking

Instructions

1. Prepare the Zucchini Noodles

   - Wash and trim the ends of the zucchini.

   - Using a spiralizer, julienne peeler, or mandolin slicer, create zucchini noodles.

2. Cook the Zucchini Noodles

   - Heat a large skillet over medium heat and add a bit of olive oil.

   - Add the zucchini noodles and sauté for 2-3 minutes until just tender. Be careful not to overcook, as zucchini noodles can become mushy quickly.

   - Season with salt and pepper.

3. Combine with Pesto

   - Add the cherry tomatoes to the skillet with the zucchini noodles.

   - Spoon the pesto sauce over the noodles and tomatoes. Toss everything together until the noodles are evenly coated.

4. Serve

   - Transfer the zucchini noodles and tomatoes to serving plates.

   - If desired, sprinkle with grated Parmesan cheese on top.

5. Optional Additions

   - You can add protein like grilled chicken, shrimp, or tofu for a more substantial meal.

   - Consider garnishing with fresh basil leaves or pine nuts for extra flavor and texture.

6. Adjust to Taste

   - Taste and adjust the seasoning as needed. You can add more pesto, salt, or pepper according to your preferences.

Gluten-Free Egg Muffins

Servings 6 muffins

1 hour

Ingredients

- 8 large eggs

- 1/4 cup milk or dairy-free alternative

- Salt and pepper to taste

- 1 cup chopped vegetables (bell peppers, spinach, tomatoes, etc.)

- 1/2 cup cooked and crumbled sausage (ensure it's gluten-free)

- Shredded cheese (optional)

Instructions

1. Preheat Oven

   - Preheat your oven to 350°F (175°C). Grease a muffin tin or use paper liners.

2. Prepare Ingredients

   - Chop the vegetables and have the cooked and crumbled sausage ready.

3. Whisk Eggs

   - In a large bowl, whisk together the eggs and milk until well combined. Season with salt and pepper to taste.

4. Add Vegetables and Sausage

   - Stir in the chopped vegetables and cooked sausage into the egg mixture. Mix well.

5. Fill Muffin Cups

   - Pour the egg mixture evenly into the muffin cups, filling each cup about 2/3 full.

6. Optional: Add Cheese

   - If desired, sprinkle shredded cheese on top of each muffin cup.

7. Bake

   - Bake in the preheated oven for about 18-20 minutes or until the egg muffins are set and a toothpick inserted into the center comes out clean.

8. Cool and Serve

   - Allow the egg muffins to cool in the muffin tin for a few minutes before transferring them to a wire rack.

9. Customize

   - Feel free to customize these egg muffins with your child's favorite ingredients, such as different vegetables, meats, or cheeses.

Sweet Potato Nachos

4 servings

40 minutes

Ingredients

- 2 medium-sized sweet potatoes, washed and thinly sliced into rounds

- 1 cup shredded cheese (ensure it's gluten-free)

- 1 cup black beans, drained and rinsed

- 1/2 cup diced tomatoes

- 1/4 cup sliced black olives

- 1/4 cup sliced green onions

- 1/2 teaspoon ground cumin

- 1/2 teaspoon paprika

- Salt and pepper to taste

- Olive oil for drizzling

- Salsa and guacamole for serving

Tools- Large bowl for tossing sweet potatoes

- Baking sheet for roasting

- Oven for baking

- Serving platter

Instructions

1. Preheat Oven

   - Preheat your oven to 400°F (200°C).

2. Prepare Sweet Potatoes

   - Wash and thinly slice the sweet potatoes into rounds.

3. Season Sweet Potatoes

   - In a large bowl, toss the sweet potato slices with olive oil, cumin, paprika, salt, and pepper.

4. Bake Sweet Potatoes

   - Arrange the seasoned sweet potato slices on a baking sheet.

   - Bake for 20-25 minutes or until the sweet potatoes are crispy and golden brown.

5. Assemble Nachos

   - Sprinkle shredded cheese over the sweet potato slices.

   - Add black beans, diced tomatoes, black olives, and green onions on top.

6. Broil Until Cheese Melts

   - Place the baking sheet back in the oven and broil for 2-3 minutes until the cheese is melted and bubbly.

Banana-Oat Cookies

12 cookies

25 minutes

Ingredients

- 2 ripe bananas, mashed

- 1 cup gluten-free rolled oats

- 1/2 cup chocolate chips (ensure they're gluten-free)

- 1/2 teaspoon vanilla extract

- 1/4 teaspoon ground cinnamon (optional)

- A pinch of salt

Tools

- Mixing bowl

- Fork or potato masher for mashing bananas

- Baking sheet

- Parchment paper or silicone baking mat

- Oven

Instructions

1. Preheat Oven

   - Preheat your oven to 350°F (175°C). Line a baking sheet with parchment paper or a silicone baking mat.

2. Mash Bananas

   - In a mixing bowl, mash the ripe bananas with a fork or potato masher until smooth.

3. Add Ingredients

   - Add the gluten-free rolled oats, chocolate chips, vanilla extract, ground cinnamon (if using), and a pinch of salt to the mashed bananas.

4. Mix Well

   - Stir the ingredients until well combined. The mixture should have a cookie dough-like consistency.

5. Form Cookies

   - Drop spoonfuls of the dough onto the prepared baking sheet, spacing them a couple of inches apart.

6. Bake

   - Bake in the preheated oven for 12-15 minutes or until the edges are golden brown.

7. Cool

   - Allow the cookies to cool on the baking sheet for a few minutes before transferring them to a wire rack to cool completely.

8. Store

   - Once cooled, store the banana-oat cookies in an airtight container.

Veggie Rice Paper Rolls

8-10 rice paper rolls

25 minutes

Ingredients

For the Rolls:

- Rice paper wrappers

- Rice noodles, cooked and cooled

- Carrots, julienned

- Cucumber, julienned

- Bell peppers, thinly sliced

- Avocado, sliced

- Lettuce or spinach leaves

- Fresh herbs (mint, cilantro, or basil)

For the Dipping Sauce:

- Gluten-free soy sauce or tamari

- Lime juice

- Honey or agave syrup

- Sesame oil

- Crushed red pepper flakes (optional)

Tools

- Large bowl with warm water for soaking rice paper wrappers

- Cutting board and knife for preparing vegetables

- Plate or surface for assembling the rolls

- Small bowl for mixing the dipping sauce

Instructions

1. Prepare Ingredients

   - Slice and julienne all the vegetables, and have the rice noodles cooked and cooled.

2. Soak Rice Paper Wrappers

   - Fill a large bowl with warm water. Dip one rice paper wrapper into the water for about 5-10 seconds until it becomes pliable.

3. Assemble the Rolls

   - Place the soaked rice paper wrapper on a flat surface.

   - Add a small amount of rice noodles, followed by a few slices of carrots, cucumber, bell peppers, avocado, lettuce or spinach, and fresh herbs.

4. Roll the Wrapper

   - Fold the sides of the wrapper over the filling and then tightly roll from the bottom, similar to a burrito.

5. Repeat

   - Repeat the process with the remaining rice paper wrappers and filling ingredients.

6. Make Dipping Sauce In a small bowl, mix gluten-free soy sauce, lime juice, honey or agave syrup, sesame oil, and crushed red pepper flakes (if using).

Quinoa Mac and Cheese

4-6 servings

40 minutes

Ingredients

- 1 cup quinoa, rinsed

- 2 cups elbow macaroni (gluten-free, if needed)

- 2 cups shredded sharp cheddar cheese (or a combination of your favorite cheeses)

- 1 cup milk (dairy or a dairy-free alternative)

- 2 tablespoons unsalted butter (or dairy-free butter)

- 2 tablespoons gluten-free all-purpose flour

- 1/2 teaspoon garlic powder

- 1/2 teaspoon onion powder

- Salt and pepper to taste

- Optional: breadcrumbs for topping

Tools

- Medium-sized saucepan

- Large pot for boiling pasta

- Whisk

- Baking dish

- Oven

Instructions

1. Cook Quinoa

    - In a medium saucepan, cook quinoa according to package instructions. Set aside.

2. Cook Macaroni

    - Cook the elbow macaroni in a large pot of salted boiling water until al dente. Drain and set aside.

3. Make Cheese Sauce

    - In the same pot used for boiling the macaroni, melt butter over medium heat.

    - Add the gluten-free flour and whisk constantly for about 1-2 minutes to create a roux.

    - Slowly pour in the milk, whisking continuously to avoid lumps.

    - Stir in garlic powder, onion powder, salt, and pepper.

    - Add shredded cheese gradually, stirring until the cheese is melted and the sauce is smooth.

4. Combine Quinoa and Macaroni

    - Add the cooked quinoa and drained macaroni to the cheese sauce. Mix until well combined.

5. Optional Breadcrumbs Topping

    - If desired, you can sprinkle gluten-free breadcrumbs over the top for a crunchy topping.

Quinoa and Veggie Stir-Fry with Chicken Strips

4 servings

30 minutes

Ingredients

- 1 cup quinoa, rinsed

- 2 cups water or chicken broth

- 1 lb chicken breast, thinly sliced into strips

- 2 tablespoons gluten-free soy sauce

- 1 tablespoon honey or maple syrup

- 2 tablespoons olive oil

- 1 bell pepper, thinly sliced

- 1 carrot, julienned

- 1 cup broccoli florets

- 2 cloves garlic, minced

- 1 teaspoon ginger, grated

- Salt and pepper to taste

- Green onions, chopped (for garnish)

Tools

- Medium saucepan with a lid

- Cutting board and knife

- Large skillet or wok

- Mixing bowl

Instructions

1. Cook Quinoa

- In a saucepan, combine quinoa and water or chicken broth. Bring to a boil, then cover and simmer for about 15 minutes until quinoa is cooked.

2. Marinate Chicken

- In a bowl, mix sliced chicken with soy sauce and honey. Let it marinate while preparing vegetables.

3. Stir-Fry Chicken

- Heat 1 tablespoon of olive oil in a skillet or wok over medium-high heat. Add marinated chicken and cook until browned and cooked through. Remove and set aside.

4. Sauté Vegetables

- In the same skillet, add another tablespoon of olive oil. Sauté garlic and ginger until fragrant.

- Add sliced bell pepper, julienned carrot, and broccoli florets. Stir-fry until veggies are tender-crisp.

5. Combine and Season

- Return cooked chicken to the skillet with vegetables. Stir in cooked quinoa. Mix until well combined.

- Season with salt and pepper to taste.

Chicken Lettuce Wraps:

Servings: 4

30 minutes

Ingredients:

- 1 lb ground chicken

- 1 tablespoon vegetable oil

- 1 onion, finely chopped

- 2 cloves garlic, minced

- 1 tablespoon ginger, grated

- 1/4 cup hoisin sauce

- 2 tablespoons soy sauce (gluten-free if needed)

- 1 tablespoon rice vinegar

- 1 tablespoon sesame oil

- 1 can (8 oz) water chestnuts, drained and finely chopped

- 1/2 cup green onions, chopped

- 1 head iceberg or butter lettuce, leaves separated

- Sesame seeds for garnish (optional)

- Sriracha or chili sauce for serving (optional)

Tools:

- Large skillet or wok

- Wooden spoon or spatula

- Cutting board and knife

- Grater for ginger

- Small bowl for sauce

- Serving platter

Instructions:

1. Prepare Ingredients:

   - Finely chop the onion, mince the garlic, grate the ginger, and chop the green onions. Drain and finely chop the water chestnuts.

2. Cook Chicken:

   - Heat vegetable oil in a large skillet or wok over medium-high heat. Add ground chicken and cook until browned, breaking it apart with a spoon as it cooks.

3. Add Aromatics:

   - Add chopped onion, minced garlic, and grated ginger to the skillet. Cook for 2-3 minutes until the onion is softened.

4. Prepare Sauce:

   - In a small bowl, mix hoisin sauce, soy sauce, rice vinegar, and sesame oil. Pour the sauce over the chicken mixture.

5. Add Water Chestnuts and Green Onions:

   - Stir in the chopped water chestnuts and half of the chopped green onions. Cook for an additional 2-3 minutes.

6. Assemble Lettuce Wraps by layering everything.

Made in the USA
Monee, IL
16 December 2024

74252600R00050